Melting

Melting

the ache of the heart
the breath of the soul

poems by george stumpf

Copyright © 2019
All Rights Reserved

No part of this book may be used or reproduced in any manner whatsoever without written permission except in the case of reprints in the context of reviews.

ISBN: 978-0-578-48412-9

Contents

Chapter 1: Splintered 9
oasis 11
Wondering 12
lonely in new york 13
the odd 14
A trace 15
Blinded 16
Two ships 17
the saboteur 18
the tsunami unseen 19
Permission 20
lovers 21
the ache of humanity 22
Your undoing 23
reckless 24
blinders 25
Wrenching in my gut 26
blood from my wound 27
the hurt i caused 28
The parting 29
So still I persist 30
unfortunately a yes 31
the breaking wave 32

the wait	33
my head and heart	34
the call	35
karma	36
I only ask for one	37
co-pilot	38

Chapter 2: Struggle ... 39

new on earth	41
glimpses of life	42
the driver	43
Each sliver	44
arms of a scale	45
an orange	46
the war	47
the nonstop	48
demanding	49
Let me peek	50
sadness of disregard	51
Too exact	52
The gardener	53
the ego	54
Unless	55
the elusive	56
no relevance	57
perception is numb	58
whatever it may be	59
Drowning	60
Steel concrete	61
To fill that void	62
the locomotive	63

narcissism	64
Fulfilled	65
the rage	66
dirt	67
modern fairytale	68
hopeless heap	69
tired	70
every night	71
the gallivant	72
It could've been	74
Self-pain	76
measuring stick	77

CHAPTER 3: RISE 79

Shooting sun	81
Slowly	82
hope	83
the freak	84
how can this not be	86
pleasure	87
an indestructible glitch	88
great art	90
the artist	91
then the skies opened	92
Inversion	93
This man	94
once a generation	95
humility	96
To live	97
Father	98
The dot of the present	99

the other night	100
The walk	101
awaiting the next day	102
like a crane	103
the real warmth	104
melting	105
I think of you	106
the genius	107
Afterword	**109**
About the author	**111**

Chapter 1

Splintered

oasis

like an oasis in the desert, so too am i
stable enough to live and to survive
enough nourishment to sustain life
but waiting—

enjoying travelers who ride the wind
honoring with feast and celebration
bidding farewell when their caravan descends
anxiously waiting—

again, comes one, a surprise passerby
a chance meeting turns to nothing

Wondering

As I am
        Walking down the street. Alone.
Thinking of the girl
        Walking down the street. Alone.
Thinking of me
        Walking down the street. Alone.

My soul mate is feeling
        Exactly what I'm feeling.
And probably at
        Exactly the same time.

Wondering when we'll finally meet.

lonely in new york

understanding what's shown in movies
walking the streets without purpose
lonely in new york

a single streetlight flickering
thinking thoughts aimlessly
hoping to find distraction

all my friends and
still i feel this way
is it love i'm missing

the odd

i'm splintered
i feel i'm just not whole

i'm injured
so i put on this façade

i go through life trying to mask the hole

but seen alone
only exasperates the odd

A trace

Writing of this hope and love and promise
Makes me introspect to find my blackness
The crevice I know has no stable steps
Only flowers sideways grow off the ledge

If ignored, grander becomes the abyss
If faced, an avalanche of loneliness
I wish to love at every path I make
Instead I peek, as love leaves but a trace

Blinded

Dreaming of ease integrated
Coupled but uncomplemented
Knowing that we're just off skewed
Blinded by benefits accrued
This list has always found success
So why now crumple in the trash

Dancing to the throbbing sunset
Erotic exploits no regret
Commingling in the native tongue
Nude unwind with the rocky sun
Awakened on the prince's isle
Coffee colored mademoiselle
Cliff jumping the ancient fortress
Waterfalling the lush forest

Raw passion excites the hunger
But prior hurt throws the dinner
Like the day's finite clock ticking
This complex affair slow dying
And though tarot says it's over
It's still sad when you turn stranger

Two ships

Two ships becoming one fleet
        the one, newly built maiden
        the second, world traveled craft

Curious of the other's hold
        combining cargo and voyage
        exploring the deep vast sea
Until a turbulent storm grew
        and tossed and waterlogged

The new, swift but unstable
        unable to grasp the sea's power
The seasoned and sea savvy
        wanting to tow the battered
        line throwing but away floating

Fate blowing in opposite directions
        sadly signals different ports

the saboteur

the mind betrays in
heart cooperation

in the abundant field of bliss
she relaxes into happiness
ease in her beau's essence

but like a stodgy historian
recalling depressed precedents
injecting them into the present

the knowing expert saboteur
can't stop slamming the door
in the face of her love adore

while deep engrained heartbroken
snide remarks and petty aversions
hammer a stake into relations

the mind finds ease in
heart destruction

the tsunami unseen

when together
we're like the yin and the yang
compliments all around
comfortable in the rain

when apart
time grows long and dark
i can feel your thoughts
the storm cloud over your heart

but the pain of the past
has drenched your whole being
throwing me aside
the tsunami unseen

Permission

I gave you permission
To be who you should be
To be your unapologetic true self

You took it and bloomed
Excited to have someone so accepting
I showed you the path and pointed out
>   the cliffs
>   the thorns
>   and the healing hot springs

But you kept getting lost
Picking the fruit from the nearby garden
Unwilling to share its succulent

Eating the destructive poison of control
Your hostility grew
Becoming more and more unfair

Was there ever respect
Or are you the master actor in this scene of love
Upstaging and condescending your way to arrogance

But I know who you really are
Afraid to get too close
Or just not knowing how

Your mouth never really could speak
Your throat rebelled at its jail
Full circle as happiness disappears

lovers

you said you were sad
it made me too

you didn't want to talk
and hung up the phone

i thought of you all day
but gave you space

i reached out once more
now you're entertaining lovers

the ache of humanity

across the room
from another table
the anguish in your eyes
seeping through

the language of your body
drowns his whispers
trying to keep invisible
the growing despair

a reprieve
most are in their own worlds
failing to see
the snowball rolling downhill

you want to cry
to plead
to kiss
his words sting
your answers muted

the perceptive outsider
straining to hear
sounds pieced together

finally giving up
he leaves
helpless

looking back one last time
your face pierces his soul
showing all the ache of humanity

Your undoing

I'm on the outside looking in.
Basking in your bittersweet win,
You stoop to hateful labeling,
Condescending and name calling.

"His grotesque urges to behave
In that sickening certain way,
Irresistible compulsion
Against his conscious ambition."

Your lonely nights, balled up sobbing,
Hysterical screams tormenting.
Overwhelmed by innate knowledge:
Your undoing, lacking courage.

The irony, we're both the same.
The pain, starting over again.

reckless

it seemed to be simmering
just under the surface
not to be shown yet
the chef sitting on the lid

then the end – venom
surprising but not
an exploding pressure cooker
coming from nowhere

looking back
all was in plain sight
the boiling pushing up
you fighting against sense

but your deep-rooted pain
forced you reckless
making you hate yourself
leaving all in ruin

too stubborn to correct

blinders

not only did you thrust it into my heart
but you took the blade and twisted

in that moment the great times became invalid
and i wondered how i was so conned

looking back i now see your track record
that i ignored because of the prize

it was written in the program plainly so
but i like a racehorse wearing blinders

was focused on the finish line

Wrenching in my gut

Feeling I'm killing a part of me
The pain wrenching in my gut
I keep telling myself it's for the best
Questioning my rational and logic

Sometimes I feel I've lightened the load
Believing better will come my way
Wishing it could have all worked out
Feeling the pain I see in your face

The hardest thing I've had to do
Don't know when it'll get easy
Wondering was it all my fault
Sadness envelopes the whole day

Now I know what others have felt
Not wanting again to start over
It seems my eyes continually
Want to burst with liquid sorrow

blood from my wound

i've yearned to call
but couldn't bring myself to pick up the phone

i've wanted to hear your voice
but knew it would only remind me

hearing that question was like
having a stake driven through my heart

the hurt i felt only compounded
by you agreeing to my answer

was that really you
that playful always affectionate creature

turning me red from the blood
that flowed from my wound

the hurt i caused

it's so hard not to think of you
the pain you felt when i said i can't
the hurt i caused keeping you in

your lover making you doubt yourself
understanding your loneliness
your belief that every person is evil

feeling your tears over miles of land
hearing your curses on incoming winds
seeing your willingness abandon you

The parting

How does one change so drastically
From when the time of love had we
To now much less is in between?

Does the passage of time push this along
Or was love blinding the eye, like the sun?
Might I be changing whether right or wrong?

I try to recall how could this be.
Had you hidden your true identity
Or have you become this recently?

And did the parting silently forebode?
Despair and doubt may have helped overthrow,
The exact reason shall never be known.

So still I persist

A weighted rope tugging at my heart
Compressing me to miniature size.
Looking for courage, maybe a gleam
Of hope for my next assaulted rise.

The pain tears at me, tears advance forth
In this mis-understandable world.
I have the right answers in my plans
But haven't found the right battlefield.

An army of emotion boils up;
Furious anger, hateful disgust
Aim to erupt but the safety's on.
Longing for calm so still I persist.

unfortunately a yes

your head on my chest
you're sobbing sad tears
i gently stroke your hair
i've been through your fears

i understand your sorrow
honored you opened your wound
i'll always be here for you
i masochistically swoon

time stops when we didn't
i could sit and enjoy
to really think about it
the future has been destroyed

too good to be true
unfortunately a yes
but i try to hold on
hope for a second chance

but it's not in the cards
you've been hurt far too deep
you've already moved on
and out of my reach

the breaking wave

the slow tide crashes low and high
trying to find comfortable time
but only in my preoccupied mind
do i feel relief

little by little the memory fades
from the dark deep i swim away
again it hits the breaking wave
i'm struggling to defeat

i grow wiser experiencing this
but it's this growth that i dismiss
my mind still murking in chaos
would give it all to have you near

your skin, your eyes, your comforting smile
reminiscing good thoughts for a while
flooding back the pain futile
bringing the undertow of tears

the wait

when it's finally stated
and the truth is evident
the future becomes uncertain

i'm lying in bed
and at last it hits me
the sadness is overpowering

i look at the trees
lost in the gaze
realize how much i love you

a bird flies by
its beauty means nothing
how could i feel so alone

keeping myself busy
not thinking of you
but the boomerang comes back

i consider its gain
it's for the best
this outweighs the first

i wake the next morning
it's a brand-new day
but the torment remains

i can only wait
for the heartbreak
to fade away

my head and heart

my head is spinning
my heart is hurting
wanting to grab the untouchable
reaching for that star invisible

my head is pounding
my heart is melting
what i want is what i see
but it seems so foreign to me

my head is unfeeling
my heart is aching
what do i have to do
to prove my worth to you

my head and heart are both crying
for another chance to redeem myself

the call

she calls
wow i was sleeping hard
why is she calling

what do i say
this is gonna be hard on us both
she just wants to hear my voice

she misses me
i miss her
words can't comfort

she's sorry she called
silence
i'm now up all night

karma

a relationship ended
while caught in the division
to make it easy on you
i knew the thing to do best

sure of myself for years
until the same befell me
and my mistake became clear
emotional shallow depth

no words to fully express
your pain many years before
like a hovering storm cloud
raining me wet with regret

while karma whispers my ear
"i never forget"

I only ask for one

A tear drops down my cheek
Something is wrong in me
Another relationship failed
Walking alone entails
Examining my soul

Why do I live if I cannot love
Why do I walk if I cannot see

To take a knife and carve out the rotten
To bare my soul but soon forgotten
Seems just like playing the lottery
The winning prize that loves completely
I only ask for one

A person as scared as I

co-pilot

i have the wheel
steering down the road
in a car that's as old as i

i seem to be getting
where i'm going
but it's always
just over the hill

my hands grow tired
they begin to look old

when the empty next seat
becomes huge
alive

pumping the pain of
no co-pilot

Chapter 2

Struggle

new on earth

knowing
but unsure how
a sphere of spirited energy
was thrust into a mass of muscle and bone

the newborn trying to adjust
to his new physical world
his soul claustrophobic

pulling at his skin
trying to loosen its hold
frustration yelling from his core

a hundred miles a minute
his mind churning
not keeping up
his tongue still learning

glimpses of life

we rare few
walk with our hearts
exposed to the world
each cut too deep to take

our senses immense
we want to be free
we want to feel completely
but we can't

and so the shell remains
only opening for glimpses of life

the driver

three years old
the mind can't comprehend
how life unfolds
from having a dad to a dead end

the rain, making a water wall
the pothole, life questionable

the bourbon, a caramel flavored gun
the embankment, the immovable won

the night, dark as bubbling tar
the driver, wrecked, the car

four years old
the mind can't comprehend
how life unfolds
from having a dream to misfortune

Each sliver

Afraid to lift the veil and show what's inside
The pieces of the core are unsettling
The ignorant label and turn their backs
Knowledge shows each sliver is known to all

arms of a scale

arms of a scale hold two stones
    the fear of rejection
    the comfort of silence
truth wins when the scale is level

but underneath the stones there's more—

something more powerful
    the calm of the spirit
    the simpleness of love
fighting the unbalanced mind

an orange

you only see my façade outside
in confident almost emotionless form
and you treat me like such

but like an orange if you peel off the rind
you find a tender sensitive core
aching to be as much

why you ask the two continually battle
because the heart wants life abundant
blind of its own and frail

the powerful mind believes it knows all
and hides the truth from the world
keeping it locked in jail

like a slave wanting freedom
but if only to kill the oppressor
or die a sad death

the war

what i should say, i don't want to
what i will say, i know your response

the should – the core of the soul's answers
the will – the yearning of man's ego

the war rages on

the nonstop

it pulls at me
it makes me sick
the knots in my stomach
have been tied by the same

it eats at me
it's on my mind
the rash on my hand
settled from the nonstop

a vicious cycle circles
until something gives
or i just give up

demanding

loving something as much as life
leads to unequivocal sacrifice
my heart knows nothing else
my mind auto-pilot continuous
as a horse follows a moving carrot
wanting someone the string to cut

yearning for the time the morsel
mouthwatering hits the tongue
marching on wearily but still
committed to do what needs to be done

wondering how exquisite the taste
and demanding it be worth the wait

Let me peek

One characteristic of myself
Which may or not be beneficial
Is that I want to try everything
And to achieve something substantial

I do all to prove my character
Then move on to bigger endeavors

I want all the world but have no time
My soul yearns what others only dream
My mind's sunflower needs to blossom
Nourishment is the knowledged sunbeam

I need experiences unique
If there's a way, at least let me peek

sadness of disregard

the world needs to know the talent the person

      will it come looking
      will i be revealed
      will the skies part

or must i force myself to be seen

      beating on my heart
      saying look at me
      with forward chest
      and outstretched arms

rain pouring the sadness of disregard

Too exact

Sometimes I can judge a person too exact,
Every idiosyncrasy, every fact.
I see things that even they might not believe,
What they're really thinking and what's up their sleeve.

This innate talent, though, might be my downfall
Because I want nothing less, perfection calls.
But what I truly see is fault and weakness,
Rendering all my relationships helpless.

I see things sooner and clearer than most see,
I don't stay long 'cause it's not healthy for me.
Am I protecting by exaggerating
And finding negative of trivial things?

The gardener

The weather and land is now optimal
Weeding through the garden bed carefully
Knowing your wants, not wanting to settle
Work weary but the belief never leaves

Sunlight glistens the flower from afar
You become awestruck as you get up close
Never-imagined beautiful flora
The gardener's hardest task… just let it grow

the ego

the downfall of every man
turns his ears deaf
his eyes blind

it makes him believe he's
bigger than life
better than others

he dodges the genuine
advancing his case
avoiding all else

but when he's dealt a bad hand
he turns looking for help
finding no friends around

realizing he's no good
this breaks him down
tears him apart

only then does his humility
come to the surface

Unless

It's always been said, you can't
        miss something you've never had
Even science says it's a fact
        unless that something is dad

There are consistent complaints
        about this oft-maligned male
But whether it's true or false
        they're able to tell the tale

My suggestion from the heart
        springs from a difficult past
Never take for granted those
        who should be close to your vest

the elusive

there is an evil side that sends me bad
but the good side tries to persuade
the two sides feud back and forth
until one commands the day

they continually pull me apart
each arguing their case
hoping every win helps them grow
stronger than their nemesis

but neither concerns my best interest
for it's the loving part that is looking
and pushing toward that cherished goal
the elusive bond between humans

no relevance

an idle mind finds time to play
imagining nonsense and disarray
i sometimes think how close am i
to falling over to the insane side

as long as i know it's aberrant
then it holds no relevance

perception is numb

waiting for the feeling
time will soon come

as it starts to happen
the mind questions the truth

more intense i sense
body over mind has won

melting to a new level
enjoying the loose

anticipation follows
my adventure's begun

everything's now a movie
reality no more

real or imagination
perception is numb

does it really matter
i'm on a six-hour tour

whatever it may be

i have all these emotions
and nowhere to put them
where is that place
who'll play that part

there is a void
that needs to be filled
some have love
some have the dark

every person
and every word
and every experience
inevitability becomes art

whatever it may be
i must find that spark

Drowning

Like a drowning swimmer
Hands grasping for help
Fighting the crashing waves
Through indifferent arms
Fiercely pushing my head
Under the water of worth
Seeing the blue sky glisten
Through the ripples clawing
Toward the breath of life

Steel concrete

Anchored to the ocean's bottom
Blasting over the clouded sky
Never parallel to the horizon
Intense emotion is the only life

Aiming to overcome the mediocre
To ascend from the lowest class
The only way is to break the ceiling
Put there by my ancestral past

To be tied to a wrecking ball
The collision of steel concrete
Will break me through or break me free
Both better that my current state

To fill that void

To cry
To rage
To feel every inch of the emotions which sustains me.

To dream
To work
To put all your energy into something that moves people.

To yearn
To hope
To fill that void that wants to be of importance.

the locomotive

the humanity of the world
has snuck up on me
like a locomotive
tearing down the tracks

its sadness
which once was hidden
has now come into the open
like the sniper's unknowing victim

its pain is sounded
through subtle hints in happy faces
and covering jokes from jovial men

the truly visceral man
knuckles the pulse of existence
by the invisible pin at his core

only then can he start
to really live
to really love
to really understand

narcissism

after years of work and affirmations
the self confident walks proudly in peace
learning to love himself, gifts back times ten
the compassion to love humanity

in the meantime here comes the discontent
the envious hateful and ignorant
picking up a sledgehammer and swinging
trying to chip away the well meaning

branding the assured yelling from rooftops
"he of low esteem the arrogant fuck
discredits belittles and ridicules
let's drag him off his pompous pedestal"

but careful with the cursed rocks you throw
as a surrounding wall begins to grow
out of the very rocks you thought hidden
imprisoning you in your own dungeon

while the sad continually betray
the actual narcissist misbehaves
the cosmos silently reaffirms faith
the undaunted confident plays the day

Fulfilled

I know how but I keep falling back
Back to the old bad ways and habits
Slowly surely I climb the ascent
Two steps forward but then back one step

Destiny is pointing to success
And I do everything to stop this
But thankfully I'm still on the path
Will I reach the peak before I pass

I can say it's got a hold of me
Now unrecognized from the journey
But changing and molding me down deep
Making me stronger definitely

Until the pain and breaking reveal
A thousand year struggle but fulfilled

the rage

the rage like a volcano
calm for a hundred years
birds and animals play around its crater
home to happiness and peace

until the core of its being is shaken
a shift in the fault opens its heart
a betrayal of the natural habitat
the eruption of angered lava

the mountain knows not what to do
with its powerful bursting emotion
ashamed but too ingrained to control it
it devastates everything in its path

and people and earth and nature
can only wait for it to simmer
wait for the magic of time
to scab the wound

dirt

frivolity is my enemy
skimming the surface of life
unaccepting of the façade
that people call love

to have something deeper
to dig a hole with my fingers
to the center of the earth
as my nails become filled with dirt

if i can't have the crystal
if i can't have soul mitosis
then i want to die alone

if i can't have spiritual pain
if i can't have encompassing love
then kill me now

modern fairytale

the cinderella fairytale
dreaming of carefree love
no cloud in the sky
butterflies are fluttering
the wind blows a whimsical melody
and all animals are dancing

the handsome prince grows weary
walking the world searching
for the beauty who melts his heart
only to stumble upon destitute
but the kind-hearted prevails
and he takes her hand to the castle

the american reality show
consorting in a bar chugging
all chained to their phones
swiping through a thousand pics
the speakers blast angry hard rock
and all the depressed are crying

the strung out partier grows jaded
leaving her friend ordering
another shot to lose control
only to stumble into a drunkard
but the slurred and jagged embrace
and he holds her head to the toilet

hopeless heap

we humans struggle with life
we yearn to die to medicate to escape
we humans hate our lives

but angrily go along heads down
for our allotted time
never being told why

is this the hell the righteous talk about
endlessly living emotional breakdowns
hoping to break the pattern and be happy

only for life to pull the rug from under us
leaving us a hopeless heap of boneless skin
praying for this eternity to end

tired

sometimes i feel i know everything
that god's hand is leading me
showing me the answers

sometimes i feel i know nothing
that my life is a guessing game
i play with myself

still searching for the answers
i should know by now

still at the starting line
yet tired as if i've run the race

every night

a death i die every night
only to be born in the morn

the long day's life again
points one clear direction

falling off the edge of time
when it pillows my head

abruptly delaying my wants
the agony of desire

the gallivant

half way home
i begin to think of the gallivant
of what was learned
and things forgotten

remembering the sad
examining the loss
disbelief of stupidity
and how i could not see

looking behind
a trail of waves
of crests and troughs
realizing i would not change a thing

but this gallivant
was long
was lonely
was hard

even now each trudging step
is steeped in knowledge
piling on an increment
every heel to ground

the focus of the eye
becomes the purpose of the step
and the reason is envisioned

but now through minutiae
the night's black challenges
the walk of sense

a faint glint through the trees
a light on the porch
the day's glow
begins to show the path

the new view
punctuates the new view
calm seeps in
while destiny closes in

It could've been

Newborns
Given an unblemished mind
And nature perfectly coincides
Curiosity creates exploration
Learning truths of this dimension

Children
Become aware of existence
Of themselves and other humans
Blindly trusting older beings
Believing theirs flawless teachings

Teens
Negative thoughts manifest
When there's no moral guidance
Building a permanent foundation
Ignorance breeding false imagination

Adults
Possessed by prejudice
From insecurities and arrogance
Poisonous energy slowly leaks
Shackled in a jacket of false beliefs

Elders
Weary from their history
Realizing hate left them empty
Wishing life were the fabled celebration
Knowing in their core it could've been

Spirits
Having an unblemished soul
Working perfectly with the cosmos
Divinity naturally enlightens
Knowing truths of all dimensions

Self-pain

I lay here thinking death would put an end
To the continuous search for a new land

> I could really live
> I would have bliss
> I could just be
> I would be free

Death melts into all – the ease of self-pain

measuring stick

like a math teacher we carry a ruler
placing in our minds this useless metaphor
its length varies and unique to its owner
determined by various social markers

a measuring stick for our generation
we then do the worst thing we can imagine
every day measuring false expectations
letting our societal place be questioned

this daily self imposed becomes a struggle
beginning in our heads then turns to battle
progressing to our body-heart visceral
the toll eventually weighs on our souls

Chapter 3

Rise

Shooting sun

The aching of the heart
Comes when you least expect it

The breath of the soul
Wondering why you've starved it

The knowing of the mind
Waits for the worlds to collide

So the feeling of the body
Can experience love the first time

The fusion of two forms one
And births a rare shooting sun

Slowly

The world waits for me but not very long
The birds are calling with beautiful song
The sun's warm beams are comfortably muting
The wind has died down listening for me
The day will go on even while I sleep
The invisible life force slowly breathes

hope

life is sad
death comes with lightning quickness
disasters are as powerful
innocent people are the unfortunate ones

truth is so rare
love is more so
tragedy is in every success
true friends are lost

depression sinks us
darkness never dies
deceit always hurts
life is sad

but hope is never fleeting

the freak

not because of his dress or conduct
but because of his thoughts
he labels himself a freak

an extreme thinker in a moderate world
thoughts have no discrimination or order
everyday occurrences are unique

what if this is done or that is said
a thousand tales run through his head
not oppressed by this reality

always being pulled apart, torn
between his mind's world
and logical morality

family demands the straight and narrow
his mind says do what he feels
but their truth is winning

is this good? he's not sure
is he scared and of what?
why is this happening?

if he reveals his true self
he becomes vulnerable
to people to society

little by little…

aspirations are created
verging on the weird
only to be met with struggle

from a lover
disbelief
sneering at the criminal

from a friend
judgment
laughing at the crazy

but still he perseveres
making love a creative outlet
by breaking walls to find the happy

and I, growing the mind from
the world that jails me

how can this not be

don't fight it
it's nirvana

go along
and you will know
the minute and insignificant
the fine line between life and non-life

your mind will try to rationalize
are aliens doing tests on you
is the government in on it
is death near

it can be better than sex
particles dissolving in front of you
everything is warmly wrapped

melting into the environment
hearing the hammer in your ear
blood flowing inside you

how can this be
how can this not be

pleasure

the want most visceral
pushing past the responsible
coloring every minute decision
turning drink from inhibition
flaming a sunset from dark disorder
framing flowers in the grown over
breaking the ordinary
kinking the missionary
turning flab to adonis
from the couch to wanderlust
flavoring the dinner table
gifting joy to the miserable

but still we must be vigilant
when leaning toward extravagance
pointing in the direction
of every fucked up addiction
should our quest be condemned
or is addiction the villain

an indestructible glitch

in light, robot zombies plod heavily
as cogs in the machine of fallacy
their unseen power chords intersect
to the outlet of false righteousness

programmed by their godly saviors
the government unscrupulous
the church sanctimonious
and petrified shameful parents

but an indestructible glitch in the system
uploads to a fraction of the federation
one shadowy off-centered eye
accompanied by an impassioned smile

and when darkness pacifies the rest
these deviants see differently the matrix
and shed the iron cloak of suppression
revealing their habit of liberation

venturing through the back alley dark
to the voluptuous forbidden garden
they come upon a celebration of spirit
where authenticity lives pre-eminent

a place where love is free from restraint
where they find judgment nonexistent
where the norm is whole-hearted acceptance
and earth's atmosphere is compassion

for a brief moment in time these zombies
feel human as they come together passionately

great art

nothing is absolute
there is no black or white
gray is the color of life
every story has three sides
and the middle is the truth

great art no matter the forms
is not convoluted indifference
but in the polar opposites
whether negatives or positives
bursting either side of discourse

the artist

the transcended
the enlightened
their soul awakened
the human exception
has wrong disposition
for creative construction

the apathetic
the unsympathetic
their heart barbaric
the human aberrant
holds incorrect climate
for theatrical statement

the typical
the egotistical
their sleeve emotional
the human actuality
breeds sound authority
for artistic possibility

the confident
the unrepentant
their view definite
the human passionate
blends perfect environment
for brilliant achievement

then the skies opened

the dream was routine
a fleeting thought of every man
most quickly vanished

but i grabbed it until it lived in me
pushing me every day through life
to build my masterpiece
patiently waiting to evolve
to fly with the few eagles

then the skies opened
and lightning struck
the energies of the world became one

i was ready to dive from the nest
to spread my wings and soar

Inversion

Life gives you inversion
Trying to meld the two
The answer lies only
On the stage of make believe
All else fades to black
As the actor becomes you

This man

Only the stupid tries the impossible
Only the idiot seeks the unattainable
Only the dreamer looks to the sky to find a star
       and builds a rocket to take him there

But it's this man who wins
It's this man who goes down in history as the genius
It's this man who has that look in his eye

once a generation

once a generation
someone is born
who takes the commonly accepted
flips it
and shows us something new
we the masses will rebel
cursing change
afraid of upsetting the status quo
this trailblazer will flourish
with a confident wicked grin
staring at the now upside down world
reveling that their view
is now ours

humility

like a blanket of snow enveloping me
and i standing there
arms raised
inviting it to come

it lifts me up
i laugh in awe at the irony
the irony i knew all the time
but pushed away

the welcoming feeling
chilling my bones
bringing me to realization

the snow of humility

To live

To captivate
>to enchant the unexpected
To be different
>to have courage to turn away from conformity
To tell a story
>to transform mundane events into exuberance

To write a poem
>to jot a rhyme by giving over to emotion
To heal the ailment
>to remedy the ills of society
To be exceptional
>to rise about all the world's mediocrity

To create
>to give birth to something out of nothing
To be available
>to open up your soul so we all become one
To be confident
>to push away all of life's insecurities

To pounce like a lion for the thing we want
To connect like a line but in unusual order
To be in awe of the beauty outside and in

To live

Father

Often I wonder how different it would be
If one thing in my life had changed for me.

If I had the power to alter my past
I would have my father minus the crash.

Knowing there were things we had never done
But understanding that he too missed the fun.

Would I've learned lessons which changed who I am?
Would I be a different person, a better man?

The things in my life, I've learned on my own.
He could have taught me all that he had known.

But what could've been is all for naught,
This inconvenience is still unfortunate.

This, my destiny, no matter who I've become,
He's looking down on me proud of his son.

The dot of the present

If the dot of the present
In our timeline reality
Was changed not to reflect
Each of our personal needs

But so as to acknowledge
Our collective wants
We could then forget this
Linear demand existence

But because we are pulled
By the desires of the soul
Of things it first must do
We rest not nor find joy

Until the stars align when destiny smiles upon us

the other night

the other night
i wanted to let you know how i felt
i didn't have the nerve

the other night
i couldn't keep my eyes off you
did you even notice

the other night
i wanted to kiss you lightly on your lips
but was afraid

the other night
i just wanted to be with you
and still you didn't know

but it's a new night
and you will know how i feel
if only i have the nerve

The walk

Why is it so hard to make conversation
    when words are so easy to speak?
Why is it difficult to approach
    when legs are so easy to move?
Is it the beauty that is seen
    in the person out of reach?
Or is it the shyness that appears in
    the person in your shoes?

And each, it feels, keeps growing
    larger in time
Until the beginning seems like
    a baby's first stride
But if this story has found
    a knot in your stomach
There's a sure-fire means to
    relieve you from flummox
It's the goading-on of that
    annoying friend at your side
Who won't leave you alone until
    you put it all on the line

awaiting the next day

i walk in oblivious
my mind in work mode
i hear the sweetest "hey"
sensory overload

i look up to see sultry eyes
looking back at me

imagining what you're thinking
while we talk all surface
that oh-so-cute beauty mark
seducing happiness

my scanning eyes scour to try
to keep my deep cover alive

but how can i not
pull you in for a kiss
when your mischievous smile
casts a line and catches this

i watch you walk away
awaiting the next day

like a crane

it happened by accident
we unlikelies not looking
hypnotized over spilled wine
fate shaping a new blueprint

loving you digs me deeper
and holds a mirror to my eyes
revealing my broken mind
showing my flawed character

but our love is demanding
as a tower crane lifts beams
repairing a building frame
so too am i high rising

the real warmth

the soul waits as the body searches

teased by beauty
the light peeking around the eclipse
only to become
the repeated false rays of time
the real warmth
the heart of its mate

patience finally unneeded

melting

to melt with someone
the common man's goal

finding a precious gem
i begin to fall

time stops while
all else becomes dull

trusting intrinsically
i see the true you as you open

i uncover a new pearl
the fall deepens

as we melt
you beautifully blossom

I think of you

When burdened with the weight of the world
I think of you to lighten the load

When my path to happiness becomes rocky
I yearn for your kisses to smooth the way

When the nights become dark and solitary
Your body by my side is the sunrise

When the days become glaring and overexposed
Your presence is the cool shade of comfort

When the silence becomes deafening
I want to hear your contagious laugh

When the noise becomes too loud
It's drowned by your calming whispers

And when my heart can't bear us being apart
I only look forward to when we're together

the genius

to be stimulated intellectually
euphoric
to be inspired emotionally
explodable
the more exciting
the more elated

it becomes addictive
like a drug

wanting more and more
i feel the genius
of how they live
where all is possible

like the well-armed soldier in battle
bringing confidence
a sense of power

power that
if harnessed
cannot be stopped

Afterword

I am honored to share Melting with you. This is all very crazy because I never actually set out to write a book nor had I ever thought that poetry would be something that would inspire me. This book is an accumulation of poems written over the years of happiness and despair. If a relationship ended or if I needed to get something off my chest, I just sat down and wrote. Last year, I pulled my writings out from under the bed and my friends made me realize that some were actually pretty good... this book is the result.

Putting words on paper really helped get me through some rough times and I'm encouraging everyone, especially those struggling with mental health issues, to do the same and share their thoughts and feelings. It doesn't have to be poetry or even writing. It can be expressed through song, dance or whatever creative outlet you want to explore. My main intention with this book is to inspire you. I am the perfect example that, if you just follow your heart, anything can be done. I challenge you to express your yourself. And please message me with updates along your journey!

About the author

George Stumpf was raised in Pennsylvania and attended Milton Hershey, a school for children from families of low income, limited resources and social need. It was there on the farm where he milked cows, paving the way to becoming a distinguished honors student, athlete, actor, writer and entrepreneur.

If you would like to leave your thoughts or are interested in updates and inspirations, you can find him on social media:

IG: meltingpoems
FB: melting.poems
TW: meltingpoems

www.ingramcontent.com/pod-product-compliance
Lightning Source LLC
Chambersburg PA
CBHW051406290426
44108CB00015B/2172